This edition published by Barnes & Noble, Inc.,

2002 Barnes & Noble Books

ISBN 0-7607-3154-3

First published in Great Britain in 1999 by Brimax
an imprint of Octopus Publishing Group Ltd
2-4 Heron Quays, London, E14 4JP
© Octopus Publishing Group Ltd.

Printed and bound in China

2 4 6 8 10 9 7 5 3 1

My First Prayers

- All Things Bright and Beautiful
- All Things Great and Small
- All Things Wise and Wonderful
- The Lord God Made Us All

Illustrated by Stephanie Longfoot

BARNES
& NOBLE
BOOKS

We are your little children;
To you, dear God, we pray.

Keep us safe through every day
In all we do, both work and play.

Help us when we cross the street
To think of others – take their hands.

Help us get to know and love
Those from other lands.

When the sun has gone to bed
And it's our bedtime, too,

Watch over us while we're asleep,
Dear God, we pray to you.

Teach us to remember that
We can help everywhere,

And look after the little things
Who need our love and care.

Show us, we pray, dear God,
How to share our toys;

Love us always, help us try
To be good girls and boys.

God Bless Mother, who looks after us
All day and night time too.

God Bless Daddy, who takes care of us
And shows us what to do.

God bless our home. May everyone
Keep well and warm inside.

God bless our pets. Look after them
Should they run off and hide.

God bless our land: the trees, the sky,
The birds that sweetly sing.

God bless each flower that grows
And every living thing.

God bless those we see each day.
Keep us safe in all our play.

God bless sick children – make them well,
To you, dear God, we pray.

God bless children everywhere;
Teach us to love each other.

Show us how to live and share
Like sisters and like brothers.

Everything that we can see
God made for us – for you and me:

Sun and rain so things can grow,
Trees and flowers – seeds we sow.

The tiny mice; the goldfish;
The kitten at it's play;

Birds that fly; puppy dogs
Running around all day

Cows and ponies in the fields;
Bees and butterflies;

Baby lambs that run and skip
Under sunny skies.

God made the sky, the moon, the stars;
So we give thanks to Him.

He made the seas where boats can sail
He made all the fish that swim.

We ask him to help others
Who cannot see or walk at all;

And we will help them for His sake
Because God made us all.

Thank you for each morning that
We wake to a new day.

Thank you for the friends we have,
Our games and fun and play.

Thank you for the winds that blow,
Tossing leaves on high.

Thank you for the sun and clouds,
Racing through the sky.

Thank you for good-tasting food,
For eggs and fish and meat;

Thank you too for lovely fruits,
Ripe and full and sweet.

Thank you for each drop of rain
And thank you, God, for puddles.

Thank you for our special pets
Who come up close for cuddles.

Thank you for the silver moon,
The stars that shine and peep.

And when the day is over
We thank you for our sleep.